1 9 8 7
The Year I Was Born

Compiled by Sally Tagholm

Illustrated by Michael Evans

in association with Signpost Books

FANTAIL PUBLISHING, AN IMPRINT OF PUFFIN ENTERPRISES
Published by the Penguin Group
Penguin Books Ltd, 27 Wrights Lane, London W8 5TZ, England
Penguin Books USA Inc., 375 Hudson Street, New York, NY 10014, USA
Penguin Books Australia Ltd., Ringwood, Victoria, Australia
Penguin Books Canada Ltd, 10 Alcorn Avenue, Toronto, Ontario, Canada
M4V 3B2
Penguin Books (NZ) Ltd, 182–190 Wairau Road, Auckland 10, New Zealand
England
Published by Penguin Books in association with Signpost Books

First published 1992
10 9 8 7 6 5 4 3 2

Based on an original idea by Sally Wood
Conceived, designed and produced by Signpost Books Ltd, 1992
Copyright in this format © 1992 Signpost Books Ltd.,
25 Eden Drive, Headington, Oxford OX3 0AB
England

Illustrations copyright © 1992 Michael Evans
Text copyright © 1992 Sally Tagholm

Editor: Dorothy Wood
Art Director: Treld Bicknell
Paste up: Naomi Games

ISBN 1 874785 07 4 Hardback edition
ISBN 0140 90370 4 Paperback edition

Colour separations by Fotographics, Ltd.
Printed and bound in Belgium by Proost Book Production through
Landmark Production Consultants, Ltd.

Typeset by DP Photosetting, Aylesbury, Bucks

MY FAMILY

ME

Name: Timothy
Date of birth: 22 Sep 1987
Time of birth:
Place of birth:
Weight at birth:
Colour of eyes: grey
Colour of hair (if any): brown
Distinguishing marks:

SISTER/BROTHER

January

Thursday
January 1

Bank Holiday. London's first-ever New Year's Day Big Parade: 11 bands with more than 2000 musicians from Europe and America march along Piccadilly and up Regent Street.

Friday
January 2

'Celebrating Age' Year starts today. The British team in the 9th Paris–Dakar road rally arrives safely in Barcelona even though they lost a wheel at 129km/h, high in the Pyrenees.

Saturday
January 3

The International Union of Conservation of Nature and Natural Resources launches a search for a rare freshwater cod called the burbot, last seen ten years ago.

Sunday
January 4

240 people take part in the annual Pooh-sticks race under the bridge at Little Wittenham, Oxfordshire.

Monday
January 5

Tower Bridge closes to traffic for 2hrs after the gib of a crane being carried down the river on a barge crashes into the overhead walkway at 5.20pm.

Tuesday
January 6

Twelfth Night: take down your Christmas decorations! Ebb, a rare Bengal eagle owl, who escaped from a falconry nr Kidderminster, Worcs., is caught and taken home to his mate Flo.

Wednesday
January 7

St Distaff's Day: back to work after the Christmas holidays! Watch out for bird tables sprouting in north London: Camden Council are giving them to elderly, housebound tenants as New Year presents!

Thursday
January 8

The Royal Mint unveils the new English version of the £1 coin, showing an oak tree. It's the last in a series for each part of the United Kingdom.

Friday
January 9

Restoration work begins on the 1000-year-old Ely Cathedral in Cambridgeshire.

Saturday
January 10

23 football matches are cancelled because of bad weather. It's so cold in Sweden that people are advised not to wash!

Sunday
January 11

First major snowfalls all over the country. It's –3.3°C in London, the coldest January day since records began! Annual Husky Sled Dog Rally in Sherwood Forest, Notts.

Monday
January 12

Plough Monday. More snow all over the country. It's so cold that Big Ben's chimes freeze! The train which left Charing Cross for Dover at 10.30pm last night reaches Ashford, Kent, at mid-day today. –15.9°C at Aviemore and –15.5°C at East Hoathly, Essex

January

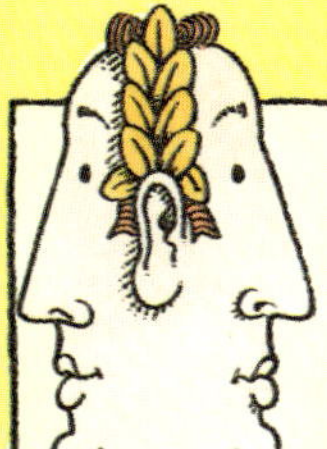

Named after the Roman god Janus, who had two faces and could look backwards and forwards at the same time; also known as 'frosty-month', 'after-yule', 'first-month' and 'snow-month'.

Chinese Year of the Cat

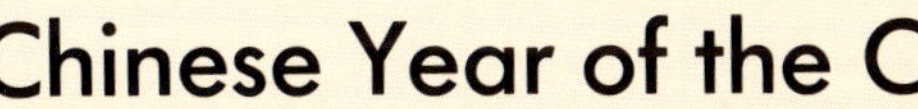

According to legend, the Buddha summoned all the animals in the world to him one New Year, and promised them all a reward. Only twelve obeyed and he gave them each a year: the Rat arrived first so he got the first year! The order of the 12-year cycle is always the same: Rat, Buffalo, Tiger, Cat, Dragon, Snake, Horse, Goat, Monkey, Cockerel, Dog and Pig.

Cats are usually very happy and land on their feet! Although they are often calm and cautious, they love being with other people and adore parties. But most of all they love comfort! Cats get on well with Goats, Dogs and Pigs but NOT with Cockerels, Rats or Tigers. Famous Cats include Catherine de Medici, Queen Victoria, Einstein, Stalin, Anne Boleyn and Eva Peron.

The Year of the Tiger finishes on Jan. 28. Tigers are daring and fight for what they believe is right. Usually, they are very lucky! Famous Tigers include Beethoven, Karl Marx, Marilyn Monroe and Queen Elizabeth II.

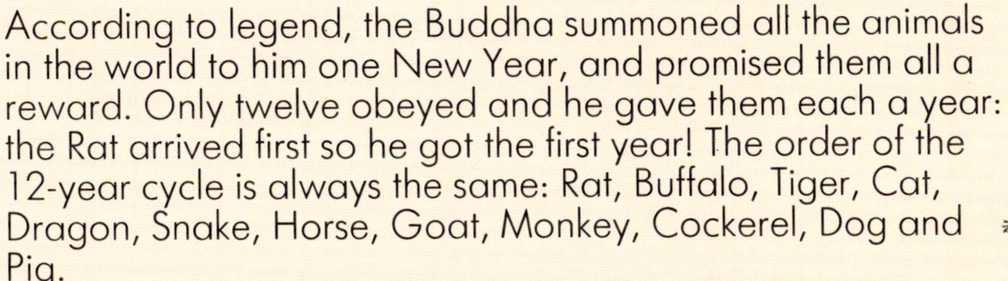

January 8: The new English £1 coin shows an oak tree on one side and the new portrait of the Queen by Raphael Maklouf on the other. It's the first time that a whole oak tree has ever been seen on a Royal Mint coin. Round the edge are the Latin words 'Decus et Tutamen' which mean 'An ornament and a safeguard'.

SSSSSSHHHHH!

The largest butter mountains are in Liverpool (22,293 tonnes) and in Bristol (17,745 tonnes). The one in London weighs only 4,137 tonnes! They all have to be kept at a temperature of –25°C. Their exact addresses are top secret in case of a national emergency.

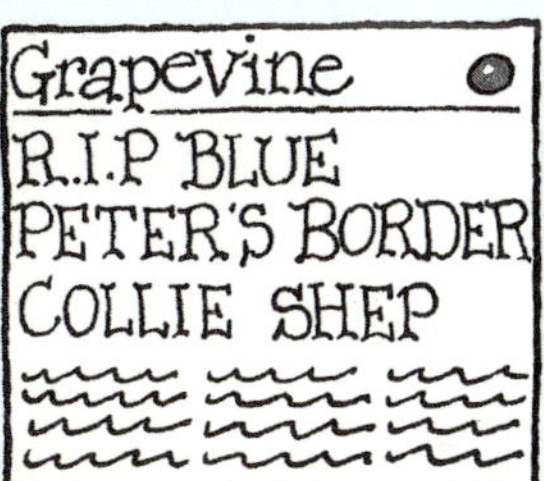

Grapevine	Good Egg	Chatterbox	Newsreel
R.I.P BLUE PETER'S BORDER COLLIE SHEP	THE ARCHBISHOP OF CANTERBURY'S SPECIAL ENVOY, TERRY WAITE, IS KIDNAPPED IN BEIRUT	MIKHAIL GORBACHEV CALLS FOR MORE DEMOCRACY IN THE SOVIET COMMUNIST PARTY	VIOLENT CLASHES BETWEEN POLICE AND PICKETS OUTSIDE NEWS INTERNATIONAL PLANT, WAPPING

| Tuesday
January 13 | St Hilary's Day—traditionally the coldest day of the year. It's so cold that British Gas sends out a record 311,300,000 cubic metres of gas to customers in the 24hrs. |

| Wednesday
January 14 | 3 Alsatian dogs called Rommel, Zeus and Zac save their owner after he falls on the ice at Barton Moss near Manchester. They keep him warm and lick his face till he regains consciousness. |

Full Moon

| Thursday
January 15 | The Mayor of Worcester takes part in an organised Sleep Out in front of the Guildhall to raise money for the homeless. He spends the night in a cardboard box. |

| Friday
January 16 | There is an acute shortage of Wellington boots nationwide. Firemen in the Forest of Dean, Gloucs., put out a fire with snowballs after their engine gets stuck in the snow. |

| Saturday
January 17 | In Belgium there's not enough snow and a World Snowman-making competition has to be put off! |

| Sunday
January 18 | A Soviet cargo spacecraft docks with the orbiting *Mir* space station and delivers supplies for a new mission. |

| Monday
January 19 | Dick Rutan and Jeana Yeager, the Americans who flew non-stop round the world in their *Voyager* aircraft, are presented with a silver medal by the Royal Aeronautical Society in London. |

| Tuesday
January 20 | The Norwegian expedition retracing Roald Amundsen's journey to the South Pole in 1911 travels at night because it is so hot. The 6°C daytime temperature is much too hot for the huskies. Firemen hack a 20m icicle off St Pancras Station, London, with axes. |

| Wednesday
January 21 | 'Cold Aid' is launched to help people who haven't got enough food in the cold weather. A 25kg block of butter is taken from one of the 98 secret depots around the country and divided up. |

| Thursday
January 22 | Californian Glenn Tremml (26), sets a new World Distance Record for human-powered flight. He pedals 59.85km (37.2 miles) in 2hrs 13mins 14secs in his extra light Eagle aircraft, which is a cross between a windmill and a bicycle. |

| Friday
January 23 | The three main reservoirs for north London have run dry after a huge amount of water is lost through burst pipes. A fleet of Thames Water tankers provides emergency supplies. |

Saturday *January 24*	The 5th annual Snow Rally in the Glenmore Forest, Aviemore. The sleds are pulled by teams of Siberian Huskies, who have fur-lined ears and webbed toes for running in the snow, and noses that go dry at night to stop them icing over!
Sunday *January 25*	The Jones family, who set off to sail round the world from Littlehampton, Sussex, in 1982 are rescued off the coast of Mexico by the liner *Canberra*. Their 10.67m ketch *Dorothy Ann* sank after they had sailed 48,270km.
Monday *January 26*	Australia Day. An 8.165kg salmon is caught on the River Wye between Ross-on-Wye and Monmouth on the first day of the salmon fishing season.
Tuesday *January 27*	A huge ticker-tape parade in New Jersey welcomes home the New York Giants after winning the American Football Superbowl. They beat the Denver Broncos 39–20.
Wednesday *January 28*	Jacky Fréon (38) of the Hotel Lutétia, Paris, wins a competition to find the best cook in the world in Lyons, France, with his '*Fine volaille de bresse aux richesses de France*'.

New Moon

Thursday *January 29*	Beginning of the Chinese Year of the Cat. Swans and ducks on the River Ouse, Cambs, turn pink when dye is spilled into the water.
Friday *January 30*	The Princess of Wales is made an Honorary Freeman of the City of London. She now has the right to drive sheep across London Bridge and can set up her own market stall!
Saturday *January 31*	It's been one of the warmest Januarys in Iceland for years: farmers are harvesting the hay already and the potatoes are sprouting!

January 20: PO issues four new flower stamps

18p
Gaillardia

22p
Echinops

31p
Echeveria

34p
Colchicum

February

Sunday *February 1*	An AA yellow and black wooden callbox built in 1932 on the A591 nr Grasmere, Cumbria, is listed as a Grade II building of architectural and historical interest. There are only 47 of them left.
Monday *February 2*	Repair work starts on the A371 into Weston-super-Mare, Avon, after badgers cause thousands of pounds of damage by burrowing into the embankment. A special pipe is being put under the road so they can cross safely.
Tuesday *February 3*	A colony of rare crested newts is saved from the bulldozer when an 11th century moat at Quedgeley, Gloucs., is declared a national monument.
Wednesday *February 4*	Britain's first commercial algae farm is opened at Reading: it can produce 2gm of algae per sq/m each hour.
Thursday *February 5*	A satellite is launched from the Kagoshima Space Centre, Japan, to search out black holes and neutron stars in deepest space. The instruments on board were designed by researchers at Leicester University.
Friday *February 6*	Mrs Margaret Thatcher's 2836th day at No 10 Downing St. She's been Prime Minister for longer than anyone else since World War II.
Saturday *February 7*	Alun Barrett (19), from Maidenhead, Berks, sets a new world record for free-fall canoeing. He drops 15.85m over Swdyn Eira (Waterfall of the Snow) on the River Hepste in South Wales.
Sunday *February 8*	Adrian Moorhouse (22), from Leeds, becomes the first man ever to swim the 100m breaststroke in less than a minute. He beats the world record by 0.25secs with a time of 59.75secs.

Monday *February 9*	British Record Industry Award for the best British group goes to 'Five Star'—five brothers and sisters from Romford.
Tuesday *February 10*	The World Wildlife Fund launches a scheme to re-establish the large blue butterfly in Britain by importing eggs and adult butterflies from Sweden.
Wednesday *February 11*	Prince Andrew takes his seat in the House of Lords as Baron Killyleagh, Earl of Inverness and Duke of York.
Thursday *February 12*	The Duchess of York is presented with her 'wings' at a ceremony at Kidlington Airport, nr Oxford. She is the first woman in the Royal Family to receive a private pilot's licence.

February

The Roman month of purification. It has also been known as 'sprout kale', 'rain-month', 'month of cakes' and 'month of ravaging wolves'.

Strictly No Entry at the Crown Jewel House

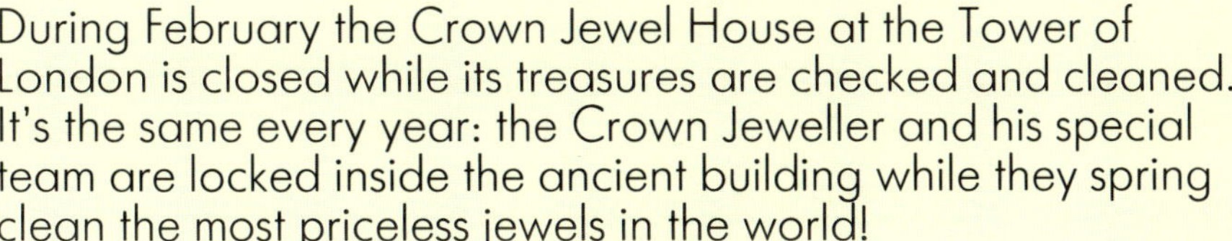

During February the Crown Jewel House at the Tower of London is closed while its treasures are checked and cleaned. It's the same every year: the Crown Jeweller and his special team are locked inside the ancient building while they spring clean the most priceless jewels in the world!

There are swords, trumpets, robes and ornaments—all the Coronation Regalia, in fact, including the largest cut diamond in the world, the First Star of Africa (530 carats). There are, of course, lots of magnificent crowns but one of the most splendid is the Imperial State Crown. You can see the Queen wearing it at the State Opening of Parliament, sparkling with more than 2800 diamonds. The Maltese Cross at the top is a sapphire said to have come from Edward the Confessor's ring and there are four large drop pearls that were probably Queen Elizabeth I's earrings! And, because it's lucky to have a red stone in a crown, it also has the Black Prince's Ruby, which was worn by King Henry V at the Battle of Agincourt in 1415—as well as the second largest diamond in the world, the Second Star of Africa (317 carats)!

SUPERNOVA 1987A

The first supernova or exploding star to be seen with the naked eye since the birth of the telescope appears in the southern hemisphere this month. It's called SN 1987A and is 170,000 light years away in the Large Magellanic Cloud. It's the first time **ever** that you can see a star in another galaxy with the naked eye. First spotted on February 23, it gets steadily brighter until May 20 and then fades quite quickly, although it goes on shining for 8 months altogether. Millions and millions of tiny neutrinos from it pass through Earth and a few are captured by special neutrino detectors. It's by far the most important astronomical event of the century!

Friday *February 13*	Choristers at St Michael and All Angels Church, Chiswick, sing all 542 hymns in the *New English Hymnal* without stopping. It takes 30hrs and they raise £2000 for charity. Full Moon
Saturday *February 14*	St Valentine's Day. The Prince and Princess of Wales launch the new European Airbus 320 in Toulouse, France. It was built jointly by France, Britain, Germany and Spain at a cost of £1.5 billion.
Sunday *February 15*	A golden-haired Afghan Hound called Champion Viscount Grant wins Best in Show title at Cruft's in London. He's 2yrs old and is known as Gable.
Monday *February 16*	Daniel Steadman (9), who plays for Moonfleet Bowling Club nr Weymouth, is chosen to play for Dorset's county bowls team.
Tuesday *February 17*	Mrs Florence Fletcher (70) of Brockworth, Gloucs., claims a record with her 87-year-old aspidistra, which was planted by her grandmother.
Wednesday *February 18*	The 13th century silver bowl discovered during excavation work at Shrewsbury Abbey, is unveiled at Rowley's House Museum, Shrewsbury. It is stamped with the earliest known assay mark.
Thursday *February 19*	Yuri Romanenko and Alexander Laveikin, two Soviet cosmonauts who were launched into space on February 6, start their first scientific experiments on board the orbiting space station, *Mir*.
Friday *February 20*	The QE2 is given a new funnel as part of a £92,000,000 refit. She is being converted from steam turbines to diesel-electric engines.
Saturday *February 21*	A mongoose called Minnie escapes from her home in north London through a cat flap.
Sunday *February 22*	Snow falls for the first time ever in the United Arab Emirates! The RSPB buys 809.38 sq km of the Campfield Marshes on the Solway estuary in Cumbria. About 10,000 pink-footed geese overwinter there each year.
Monday *February 23*	The brightest supernova (exploding star) for 383 years is spotted through a telescope at the Chilean Observatory at Las Campanas. It's the most important astronomical event of the century!
Tuesday *February 24*	Conservationists guard a colony of 30 Greater Horseshoe bats found in a barn nr Cinderford, Gloucs. They're Britain's rarest bats.

Wednesday *February 25*	The Mayor of Camden, Councillor Mary Cane, abseils down the Town Hall in aid of charity. Sub-atomic particles arrive on Earth from Supernova 1987A, which was spotted exploding on Monday.
Thursday *February 26*	The General Synod votes to allow the ordination of women priests. 
Friday *February 27*	Fifteen women deacons are ordained by the Archbishop of Canterbury in Canterbury Cathedral.

65mm of rain in Grizedale, Cumbria   New Moon

Saturday *February 28*	Bishop Robert Hardy is installed as the 70th Bishop of Lincoln in a ceremony at Lincoln Cathedral. 16°C in London

The Happy Birthday Page

Ely Cathedral is 1000 years old
Berlin is 750 years old
Chaucer's *Canterbury Tales* are 600 years old
The *Belfast News Letter* is 250 years old
Queen's Gurkha Engineers are 200 years old
St John's Ambulance Brigade is 100 years old
Football League is 100 years old
London Federation of Boys Clubs is 100 years old
Hammersmith Bridge is 100 years old
Country Life magazine is 90 years old
Transatlantic telephone service between London and New York is 60 years old
The Short Sunderland flying boat is 50 years old
National Maritime Museum at Greenwich is 50 years old
Treaty of Rome is 30 years old
New Coventry Cathedral is 25 years old
Grange Hill is 10 years old

March

Sunday *March 1*	St David's Day. A campaign to bring back skipping is launched by the Physical Education Association.
Monday *March 2*	A State of Emergency is declared in New Zealand after an earthquake on North Island measures 6.5 on the Richter Scale. There are more than 100 aftershocks.
Tuesday *March 3*	Pancake Day. The Queen presents Polar Medals to the Trans-Globe team who circumnavigated the world from Pole to Pole. Lady Fiennes is the first woman ever to receive the medal.
Wednesday *March 4*	First day of Lent. The World Wildlife Fund International launches an Emergency Appeal to save the Giant Panda. There are only about 800–1,000 left in the world now and they could be extinct in 30 yrs.

Thursday *March 5*	Womble, a 23-year-old pony, moves into the front room of a terraced house in Rhondda, South Wales, when the local council say that his stable has to be destroyed.
Friday *March 6*	Valentina Tereshkova, the first space woman, who orbited the earth 48 times in 1963, celebrates her 50th birthday.
Saturday *March 7*	A new street name, showing the City's new crest, is put up on the Bank of England today. All 2500 plates in the City of London will be replaced and the old ones sold to collectors all over the world.

Sunday *March 8*	Start of International Women's Week. Shinji Kazama, from Japan, leaves Ward Hunt Island in Canada to ride to the North Pole on a 200cc motor cycle.
Monday *March 9*	Commonwealth Day. A new avenue of 198 lime trees is planted at Hampton Court Palace, following Sir Christopher Wren's original design. They are each about 6.1m high and cost £225.
Tuesday *March 10*	Greece has its heaviest snowfall for 34 years. On the island of Rhodes, no one has ever seen snow before!
Wednesday *March 11*	The Queen unveils the first national war memorial to 1000 soldiers killed in the Korean War 36 years ago at St Paul's Cathedral.
Thursday *March 12*	The Queen's old black mare, Burmese (25), who has just retired, poses for sculptor James Osborne, who has been commissioned to make three large bronzes of her in aid of the St John's Ambulance Brigade Centenary Appeal.

March

Named after Mars, the Roman God of War. It has also been known as 'rough-month', 'lengthening-month', 'boisterous-month' and 'windy-month'.

March 6: The 7,951 tonne car ferry, the *Herald of Free Enterprise*, sets off from the Belgian port of Zeebrugge at 7pm on March 6, bound for Dover. About 600m out to sea, the ship capsizes and sinks so suddenly that there is no time to send an S.O.S. 408 passengers and crew are rescued but 189 people die in the disaster. A public inquiry is held to discover the causes of the tragedy.

R.I.P. Lancelot

This is the first winter for 24 years that Lancelot (ring number 567), the Bewick's Swan, has not been seen at the Wildfowl Trust at Slimbridge, Gloucs. His mate, Elaine, arrives back from Siberia without him just after Christmas and leaves again, alone, on March 17. It probably means that Lancelot won't be coming back because Bewick's Swans are very faithful and usually mate for life. But two more generations of his family spend the winter at Slimbridge—7-year-old Excalibur, her mate, Saxifrage, and their cygnet.

March 24: PO issues four stamps to commemorate the 300th anniversary of *Principia Mathematica* by Sir Isaac Newton

The Bugle ▲
MONSTER LAMB (7·8 KG) BORN IN TROWBRIDGE. WILTS

Daily Chuckle ●
LADY JONES IS ELECTED LIVERPOOL'S NEW LORD MAYOR.

Blurb ■
£20,000,000 TREASURE FOUND IN WRECKED SHIP OFF PLYMOUTH COAST

The World ★
GIANT CROCODILES RUIN NORTH AUSTRALIAN TOURIST INDUSTRY

| *Friday*
March 13 | Britain's first purpose-built toad tunnel under the A4155 from Henley to Marlow is opened by Lord Skelmersdale. Toads will be able to hop through it from their winter home in the woods to their breeding ponds beside the Thames. |

| *Saturday*
March 14 | The biggest known galaxy in the universe has just been found. It's a collection of stars thirteen times bigger than the Milky Way, 300 million light years away in the constellation of Andromeda! |

| *Sunday*
March 15 | A huge figurehead of Queen Victoria from the flagship *Victoria*, travels back to Plymouth by low-loader after a £15,300 facelift at Topsham, Devon. |

| *Monday*
March 16 | Schools close and nearly 2,000,000 children stay at home as more than 20,000 teachers march through the streets of London in protest at their 16.4% pay deal. |

| *Tuesday*
March 17 | St Patrick's Day. Osel Hita (2), from Grenada, Spain, is enthroned as the reincarnation of a Tibetan Lama, who died 3 years ago. |

| *Wednesday*
March 18 | Deacon Sylvia Mutch becomes the first woman in the history of the Church of England to conduct a marriage ceremony at the church of St Philip and St James, Clifton, York, at 12.15pm. |

| *Thursday*
March 19 | The guided missile destroyer, *HMS Fife*, sails up the Thames and arrives in London. She is the last ship where sailors sleep in hammocks. |

| *Friday*
March 20 | 1981 Grand National winner Aldaniti, who set off from Buckingham Palace on March 1, reaches Himbleton, nr Worcester, today. He's covering 16.1km a day in aid of the Bob Champion Cancer Trust and will arrive at Aintree, Liverpool, on Grand National Day, April 4! |

| *Saturday*
March 21 | Spring Equinox and the First Day of Spring! European Year of the Environment starts today. |

| *Sunday*
March 22 | Golden Jubilee Pioneer Run for veteran motor cycles: they cover 75.6km from Epsom Downs to Brighton. |

| *Monday*
March 23 | Designs for the three tallest skyscrapers in Europe, to be built at Canary Wharf in London's Docklands are unveiled. |

| *Tuesday*
March 24 | A 17th-century doll wearing a dress of cream, green and yellow striped silk over a brown and beige skirt, with one hand and part of a leg missing, is sold for £67,100 at Sotheby's, London. |

Wednesday March 25	The European Economic Community is 30! Heinz, the US food firm, give a 1.61km long headland called Cape Cornwall, nr Land's End, to the National Trust. It's the only 'Cape' in England!
Thursday March 26	Oranges and Lemons Service at St Clement Danes Church, London: every child is given an orange and a lemon after the service. 
Friday March 27	Gales sweep across the country at 144.7km/h. Villages in the southeast are blacked out; copper sheeting lifts off the roof of the Old Bailey, London, and the 30m spire of St James' Church, Waresley, Cambs, is demolished.
Saturday March 28	The 133rd University Boat Race is the slowest since 1979: Oxford win by 3 lengths in driving rain and choppy waters. New Moon
Sunday March 29	Mothering Sunday. There is an annular solar eclipse, when the sun makes a ring around the moon, in South America, the South Atlantic, Africa and the Indian Ocean today!
Monday March 30	Van Gogh's painting 'Sunflowers' is sold for £24,750,000 in London to Yasuda, the second biggest insurance company in Japan: it's the most expensive picture ever sold!
Tuesday March 31	Van Gogh's 'Thistles' is sold for only £286,000 at Sotheby's in London.

Top Tens of 1987

*Top Ten Names 1987**

1	Elizabeth		1	James
2	Louise		2	William
3	Mary		3	Edward
4	Charlotte		4	Alexander
5	Alice		5	Thomas
6	Emma		6	John
7	Jane		7	Charles
8	Emily		8	Christopher
9	Sarah		9	David
10	Sophie		10	George
	Victoria			

* According to *The Times* newspaper

Top Ten Films at the box office are:

1 Crocodile Dundee
2 The Living Daylights
3 Beverley Hills Cop II
4 Platoon
5 Police Academy IV
6 The Golden Child
7 Labyrinth
8 Superman IV
9 Full Metal Jacket
10 Blind Date

(BFI Information Library)

UK Fact File 1987

'Celebrating Age' Year

European Environment Year

UN's International Year of Shelter for the Homeless

Total area of the United Kingdom — 244,100 sq kms

Capital City — London (1580sq kms: population 6,770,400)

Population of UK — 56,930,000

Average population per sq km — 233

Births
775,600

Deaths
644,300

Marriages
397,900

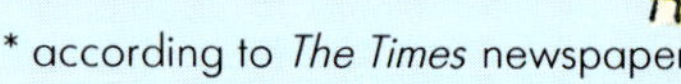

Most popular girls' name*
Elizabeth

Most popular boys' name*
James

* according to *The Times* newspaper

Head of State
Queen Elizabeth II

Prime Minister
Margaret Hilda Thatcher

Astronomer Royal
Prof. Sir Francis Graham Smith

Poet Laureate
Edward (Ted) Hughes

Archbishop of Canterbury
Robert Alexander Kennedy
Runcie

Members of Parliament
650 (523 for England, 38 for Wales, 72 for Scotland and 17 for Northern Ireland): after the General Election in June the number of women MPs goes up from 27 to 41

Presidency of EEC
Belgium (Jan–July)

Denmark (July–Dec)

Members of EEC

Belgium, Denmark, France, Federal Republic of Germany, Greece, Ireland, Italy, Luxembourg, The Netherlands, Portugal, Spain, the United Kingdom

April

Wednesday *April 1*	April Fool's Day. The Queen opens the new Turner Wing of the Tate Gallery in London and there is a firework display on the River Thames to celebrate.
Thursday *April 2*	Jewels belonging to the Duchess of Windsor, the widow of the Duke (formerly Edward VIII) who died last year, are sold in Geneva. Her emerald and diamond engagement ring fetches £1,193,408.

50mm of rain at Princeton, Devon

Friday *April 3*	Wanted: good home for a billygoat called Arthur who was found by the RSPCA wandering on the M27 near Southampton.
Saturday *April 4*	Clowns from all over the world meet at the International Clown Convention at Bognor Regis, Sussex today. There's a special procession that starts at 10.30am.
Sunday *April 5*	Arsenal wins the Littlewoods Cup Final at Wembley, beating Liverpool 2–1.
Monday *April 6*	A competition to design a fountain for Parliament Square, London, is launched today. It will be called The Queen's Fountain.

Floods in SW England

Tuesday *April 7*	World Health Day. The Official Monster Raving Loony Party has its first ever victory, winning a seat on Ashburton Town Council, Devon.
Wednesday *April 8*	The Co-op puts a special Health Warning on all their own brand sweets—like jelly beans, wine gums, dolly mixture and humbugs.
Thursday *April 9*	Dr John Pickup (39) from Guy's Hospital in London is named Doctor of the Year: he has developed a new way of controlling diabetes.
Friday *April 10*	A 27.43m high hot-air balloon, which holds 2,547 cubic metres of air, makes its test flight nr Bristol. It's in the shape of the Rosebud Egg, which was made by Fabergé and given by Tsar Nicholas II of Russia to his wife, Alexandra, on Easter Day 1895.

Saturday *April 11*	Soviet cosmonauts Yuri Romanenko and Alexander Laveikin go for a space walk that lasts over 3½ hours to help the space module *Kvant* to dock. It has tried twice before—unsuccessfully.
Sunday *April 12*	More than 1500 people attend a memorial service in Southampton to mark the anniversary of the sinking of the *Titanic* in 1912. It's the first service to be held since the wreck was found.

| *Monday*
April 13 | A special exhibition, 'Australia 200', opens at the National Maritime Museum, Greenwich, to mark the 200th anniversary of the sailing of the first settlers to Australia. |

Full Moon

| *Tuesday*
April 14 | First day of Passover. The first 3 women pilots to be employed by British Airways hold a press conference in the cockpit of a Boeing 747. |

| *Wednesday*
April 15 | Ash Wednesday. Buckingham Palace is going to have two new blue police sentry boxes at the front gates. They will be armour-plated, with bullet-proof glass. |

| *Thursday*
April 16 | Maundy Thursday. The traditional Maundy Service is held in Ely Cathedral, Cambs. The Queen presents special Maundy money to 122 pensioners—a man and a woman for each of her 61 years. |

| *Friday*
April 17 | Good Friday. Hot Cross Bun Ceremony at the Widow's Son Inn, Devons Road, Bromley. Men's British Marbles Championship at Tinsley Green, near Crawley, Sussex. |

| *Saturday*
April 18 | Square-rigged ships assemble in London Docks and get ready to sail to Australia to commemorate the 200th anniversary of the first settlers' journey. |

| *Sunday*
April 19 | Easter Sunday. Sixty floats take part in the Easter Parade in Battersea Park, London. Morecambe in Lancashire is invaded by 5500 scooters. |

| *Monday*
April 20 | Bank Holiday. Mark Ryder (26) from Abbeydale, Gloucs., wins the World Eel Eating Championship for the 5th year running. He eats 453.6g of elvers in 32secs at Frampton-on-Severn, Gloucs. |

| *Tuesday*
April 21 | Happy 61st birthday to the Queen! Shinji Kazama (36), from Japan, reaches the North Pole on a 200cc motor cycle: he's ridden 2011km from northern Canada. |

| *Wednesday*
April 22 | The final bit of the South West Peninsula Coast Path, between Barnstaple and Bideford, is opened. It stretches 869km from Minehead, Somerset to Land's End and back to Poole, Dorset. |

| *Thursday*
April 23 | St George's Day. Richard Branson launches The Forest of London Project to plant 1,000,000 trees. He climbs the tallest tree in London, a 61m plane tree in St George's Gardens, Mayfair, in 35mins. |

April

The opening month—from the Latin 'aperire' which means to open. Also known as the time of budding, the cuckoo's May or the fool's May.

THE MEN'S BRITISH MARBLES CHAMPIONSHIPS

Traditionally, the Marbles Season in Sussex runs from Ash Wednesday to 12 noon on Good Friday. The British Marbles Championships began in 1932 and has been played outside the Greyhound Pub, Tinsley Green, ever since. This year, 25 teams compete and the title is won by the Black Dog Boozers, from Crawley, for the third year running.

The ring is 6ft in diameter and about 2ins off the ground. It's covered with sharp sand before play starts. 49 marbles are used as targets and competitors take it in turn to shoot their tolleys at them and drive them out of the ring.

1962: glass marbles were used for the first time because of a shortage of traditional clay ones. The new marbles were stove enamelled red so that spectators could follow the game more easily!

'Wee Willie Wright', who used to play for the Tinsley Tigers, had a secret hot water bottle sewn inside his coat to keep his thumb warm!

The shooting marble is known as the 'tolley' and is used to knock other marbles out of the ring.

Names for the targets in marbles: Kemmies, Nibs, Commies, Crockies, Peewees, Dibs, Hoodles, Immies, Ducks, Commons, Stickers, Miggs.

Tolleys are ¾inch in diameter and targets are ½inch.

Fudging, Cabbaging and Blocking NOT allowed!

Early Victorian marbles games include Boss-out, Ho-go, Holy-Bang and Plum Pudding.

Friday *April 24*	Dust devil at Towy Castle, Dyfed. Mornington Crescent Underground station, London, becomes a Grade 2 listed building. 
Saturday *April 25*	Start of Environment Week. 8000 peace campaigners form a human radiation symbol during a Nuclear Free Rally in Hyde Park, London.
Sunday *April 26*	Paratroopers, who left Inverness 10 days ago, arrive in Aldershot after marching and running 1931km to raise money for the NSPCC and the British Heart Foundation.  New Moon
Monday *April 27*	Five square-rigged ships sail under Tower Bridge, London, at the start of a 20,113km journey to Australia exactly 200 yrs after the first settlers set off. Six other ships will join the fleet at Portsmouth. 
Tuesday *April 28*	Special announcement. The Department of the Environment says that, so far, about 3000 toads have used the tunnel under the Henley to Marlow road in Bucks, opened on March 13.
Wednesday *April 29*	The QE2 sets sail from Southampton to New York after a £92,000,000 refit.
Thursday *April 30*	First day of Ramadan. The Eve of Beltane (bright fire), the Celtic festival of the beginning of summer. Hobby Horse Celebrations start in Minehead, Somerset, at 5.30pm. Warmest April in Oxford since 1944!

ENDANGERED SPECIES IN 1987 (according to WWF)

Pygmy hippopotamus	Splendid Pearlfish
African slender-snouted crocodile	Red-headed Sideneck Turtle
Dwarf Olive Ibis	Purple-winged Ground Dove
Maroon pigeon	Golden-tailed Parrotlet
Yellow-footed Honeyguide	Helmeted Woodpecker
Western Wattled Cuckoo-Shrike	Long-Wattled Umbrella bird
Dappled Mountain Robin	Golden Toad
Brown Howler Monkey	Hercules Beetle
Woolly Spider Monkey	Natterer's Longwing
Giant Armadillo	Christmas Frigate Bird
Spectacled Bear	Slender-billed Flufftal

May

Friday *May 1*	Two cross-channel ferries collide in thick fog outside Dover harbour.
Saturday *May 2*	One of the rarest wild flowers in Britain, the Snake's Head Fritillary, blooms at Fox Fritillary Meadow, Framsden, Suffolk.
Sunday *May 3*	Hands Across Britain: people hold hands to form a human chain between London and Liverpool at 3pm to draw attention to the plight of the unemployed.
Monday *May 4*	Bank Holiday. Two French pilots become the first people to land at the North Pole in an ultra-light aircraft.
Tuesday *May 5*	Twelve poets read their work on Waterloo Station, London, during the rush hour to launch a two week 'Poetry Live' festival.
Wednesday *May 6*	Police advise families in Leicestershire, Bedfordshire and Northamptonshire to stay indoors today because of a 72km long chemical cloud in the sky.
Thursday *May 7*	The Duchess of York loops the loop in a Red Arrows Bulldog training aircraft at RAF Scampton, nr Lincoln.
Friday *May 8*	The Queen and the Duke of Edinburgh arrive in Taunton, Somerset. It's the first official visit from a reigning monarch since 1497, when Henry VII fined the town £450 for supporting the Cornish rebellion.
Saturday *May 9*	400m of green carpet (2m wide) is laid over the cobblestones along Tower Wharf by the River Thames in London to help the Marathon runners who will run along there tomorrow.
Sunday *May 10*	More than 22,000 runners take part in the London Marathon; Hiromi Taniguchi, from Japan wins in 2hrs 9mins 50secs. Ingrid Kristiansen from Norway, wins the women's race for the third time in 2hrs 22mins 48secs.
Monday *May 11*	National Speak Week is launched. The Prime Minister, Margaret Thatcher, calls a General Election for June 11.
Tuesday *May 12*	The Palm House at Bicton Gardens, nr Sidmouth, Devon, is re-opened by Lord Montagu of Beaulieu after being restored.

Full Moon

Wednesday *May 13*	Eleven square-rigged sailing ships set off from Portsmouth in a re-creation of the voyage of the First Fleet, which carried the first 1350 settlers to Australia. They'll arrive in time for Australia's 200th birthday celebrations next January.
Thursday *May 14*	The Prince of Wales spends a few days working with crofters on the island of Berneray in the Hebrides. He helps to plant potatoes and cut peat, as well as fishing and rounding up lambs.
Friday *May 15*	The Soviet Union launches a new kind of giant rocket called *Energia*, which will carry shuttles into orbit, from the Baikonur space complex.
Saturday *May 16*	Coventry City beats Tottenham Hotspur 3–2 in the FA Cup Final at Wembley. Beginning of National Wildflower Week.
Sunday *May 17*	250,000 people welcome the FA Cup winners back to Coventry. The Cathedral bells are rung for the first time in 100 years.
Monday *May 18*	Cyclist Malcolm Elliott wins the first stage of the Milk Cup Race from Newcastle to Newton Aycliffe (166km).
Tuesday *May 19*	The Labour Party election manifesto is launched at 9am. The Conservative Party election manifesto is launched at 11am.
Wednesday *May 20*	RSPB keeps round the clock watch on the secret nesting place, somewhere in the Lake District, of England's only breeding pair of Golden Eagles.
Thursday *May 21*	An unmanned cargo craft docks with the orbiting Soviet space station *Mir* and delivers food, water, fuel and equipment to Yuri Romanenko and Alexander Laveikin, who have been in space since February 6.
Friday *May 22*	A Mozart manuscript containing nine symphonies is sold for £2,585,000 at Sotheby's in London.
Saturday *May 23*	The first ever Rugby World Cup begins in New Zealand. A record price of £14,700 is paid for an angora goat at a sale at Longhope, nr Gloucester.
Sunday *May 24*	Karate instructor Paul Lynch (28), from Balham in London, claims a world record by doing 29,753 press ups in 24hrs.
Monday *May 25*	Bank Holiday. Outbreak of wilt in Hereford, Worcester and Shropshire: hop farms are put into quarantine by the Ministry of Agriculture to stop the fungus from spreading.

Tuesday *May 26*	Brian Cornwell (30) sets out from Redhill, Surrey, to push a supermarket trolley 644km along the South Coast to Land's End to raise money for the Royal Marsden Hospital, Sutton.

New Moon

Wednesday *May 27*	The Queen unveils a special plaque at the Elephant Gate in Berlin Zoo during her visit to celebrate the city's 750th birthday.
Thursday *May 28*	Mathias Rust (19), from West Germany, flies a four-seater Cessna aircraft through Russian air defences from Helsinki and lands in Red Square, Moscow.
Friday *May 29*	Richard Branson is presented with the Segrave Trophy for his record-breaking powerboat crossing of the Atlantic last summer.
Saturday *May 30*	Kevin Forster (28), from Gateshead, wins the Stockholm Marathon in 2hrs 13mins and 52secs.

Sunday *May 31*	The first aircraft lands at the new City Airport, London. Prayers are said for Terry Waite, who is 48 today, and who went missing in Beirut on January 20.

May

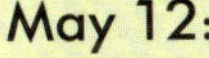

Takes its name from Maia, the goddess of growth and increase, or from 'maiores', the Latin word for elders, who were honoured this month. The Anglo Saxons called it 'thrimilce' because cows could be milked three times a day now. An old Dutch name was 'bloumaand' which means blossoming month.

NATIONAL FLOWER WEEK

May 16–25 is a busy week for bluebells, buttercups and cowslips—not to mention daisies, primroses and ragged robin. It's National Wildflower Week and there are special events all over the country. Settlebeck High School, Sedburgh, wins first prize with a daisy chain that measures 225m 60cm! During the week the 1987 Orchid Wardening Scheme and a new nationwide Waterlily Survey are launched.

May 12:   PO issues four new Europa stamps to celebrate British Architects in Europe

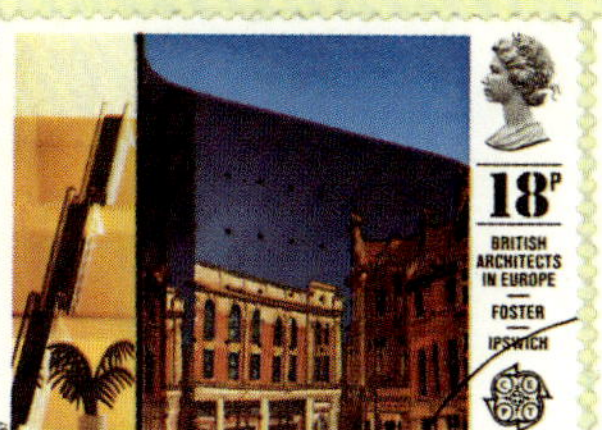

June

Monday June 1

New-coloured Postal Orders are issued with a full-face picture of the Queen instead of a side view. A baby gorilla called Kamili (Swahili for 'perfect') is born at London Zoo.

Tuesday June 2

A tiny water colour called 'Farm Building in Norfolk' by Arthur George Carrick goes on show at the Royal Academy's Summer Exhibition. It's really by the Prince of Wales, whose middle names are Arthur George. He is also the Earl of Carrick!

Wednesday June 3

Reference Point, ridden by Steve Cauthen, wins the 208th Derby at Epsom.

Thursday June 4

Eve Jackson (28), who took off from Biggin Hill, Kent, 13 months ago, lands at Darwin, Australia, becoming the first person ever to fly from Britain to Australia in a microlight.

Friday June 5

Henry, a French tight-rope walker, sits on a chair balanced on the edge of a 70.41m cliff at Cap Blanc Nez, near Calais, and looks out over the English Channel.

Saturday June 6

Police frogmen swim up and down the canals in Venice as part of a massive security operation before a seven-nation economic summit opens on Monday.

Sunday June 7

Princess Anne and her son Peter (10) both take the controls of a 6.4m inflatable lifeboat as part of a 45-minute rescue exercise in the Solent, off Lymington, Hants.

Monday June 8

For Sale: Brent Tor, an Iron Age earthwork, 405m high on the western edge of Dartmoor, Devon.

Tuesday June 9

St Columba's Day: luckiest day of the year in Highland Scotland. Professor Douglas Henderson is appointed the Queen's Botanist in Scotland. The position has been vacant for nine years.

Wednesday June 10

Happy 66th birthday to the Duke of Edinburgh! The King's Troop Royal Horse Artillery fires a salute in Hyde Park, London.

Full Moon

Thursday June 11

St Barnabas' Day. General Election: polling booths are open from 7am to 10pm. The Conservatives win 375 seats, Labour wins 229, the Liberals 17 and the SDP 5 seats.

Friday June 12

Yuri Romanenko and Alexander Laveikin make their second space walk from the orbiting space station *Mir*. They fix a panel onto the surface of *Mir* which will be used for solar batteries.

June

Takes its name from Juno, the great Roman goddess of the Moon or from 'Juniores', the Latin word for young people, who were honoured this month. 'Zomer-maand' in Old Dutch (summer month) and 'Seremonath' in Old Saxon (dry month).

The Canine Member for Sheffield Brightside

Teddy the guide dog, who is 11yrs old, has just started a brand-new life in London and taken his place in Parliament at the feet of David Blunkett, the new Labour MP for Sheffield Brightside. Although there have been blind Members of Parliament before, Teddy is the first dog **ever** to be allowed in the Chamber of the House of Commons. (He was also the first dog to be allowed up into the Gallery a few years ago.) Having lived most of his life in Sheffield, he is now having to get used to the sights and smells of London, not to mention the London Underground system.

Teddy is a cross between a curly coat retriever and a labrador, weighs more than 176kg and is a vegetarian. He lives on a special all-cereal diet with pills to protect his teeth. He was trained at the Bolton Centre run by the Guide Dog Association and started work when he was two. He will probably retire next year, when he is twelve, and will live in Sheffield with foster parents.

June 16: PO issue four new stamps to commemorate the centenary of the St John Ambulance Brigade

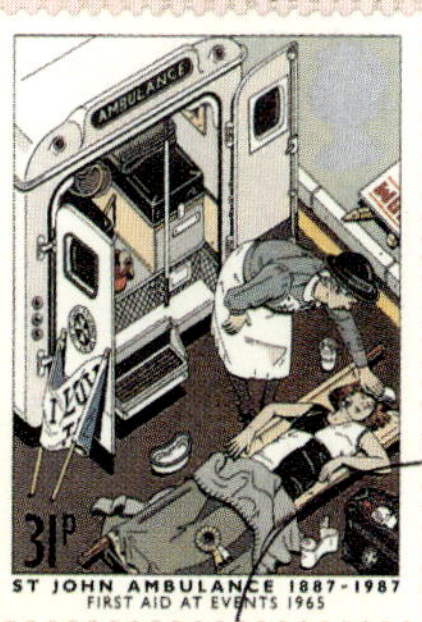

Saturday *June 13*	The Queen's Official Birthday: for the first time she takes the salute on Horse Guard's Parade from a carriage. Princess Anne is created Princess Royal for her work for children in need.
Sunday *June 14*	David Gander (32) from London, pulls Concorde (92.46 tonnes) 12.19m across the tarmac at Heathrow Airport. He raises £20,000 for the St John Ambulance Brigade Centenary Appeal.
Monday *June 15*	18,350,000 people watch 'It's a Knockout' on television: Prince Edward hosts the charity show. The Duke and Duchess of York and the Princess Royal take part.
Tuesday *June 16*	Tom McClean (44) sets out from Newfoundland to row the Atlantic for the second time. He's also sailed across it twice!
Wednesday *June 17*	So far, it's rained every day this month—it's the wettest summer for 25 years! The new Lord Chancellor, Sir Michael Havers, takes his seat in the House of Lords wearing his three-cornered tricorn hat back to front.
Thursday *June 18*	The 71.12cm Great Equatorial Telescope, the largest refractive telescope in Britain, opens to the public at Greenwich Observatory.
Friday *June 19*	Torrential rain: Gay Kelleway (23) becomes the first woman ever to win a race at Royal Ascot. She is first past the post in the Queen Alexandra Stakes on Sprowston Boy (12–1).
Saturday *June 20*	100,000 children go to a party in Hyde Park, London, to celebrate the St John Ambulance Brigade's 100th birthday. The longest sausage ever made is cooked and eaten. It measures 8.85km!
Sunday *June 21*	Summer solstice: it's the longest day of the year with the sun rising at 3.47am. 30,000 cyclists take part in the 1987 London to Brighton Bike Race.
Monday *June 22*	First day of the 101st Wimbledon Lawn Tennis Championships but there is no play because of torrential rain.
Tuesday *June 23*	Rain delays play at Wimbledon for the second day running. The Burford Dragon Procession starts at 6.30pm in Burford, nr Oxford. It commemorates the victory of the King of Mercia over the King of Wessex in 782 AD.
Wednesday *June 24*	Midsummer's Day. Watch out for swarms of huge mosquitoes in East Anglia and South East England because it's been so warm and wet!

Thursday *June 25*	Alan Hackett (29), from New Zealand, jumps from the second floor of the Eiffel Tower (116.5m) with his feet tied to a long piece of elastic. It's called 'bungy jumping', which is rather like being a human yo-yo, and he's left dangling 2.6m above the ground! New Moon
Friday *June 26*	A half bottle of Chateau Margaux 1784, reserved for the American President Thomas Jefferson, is sold for £20,000 at the Bordeaux Wine Fair.
Saturday *June 27*	The Duke and Duchess of York unveil a BR 125 locomotive which is called 'York'. It shows their combined arms for the first time—including a bee, a wreath of white roses of York and an anchor.
Sunday *June 28*	Celebrations in Brussels to mark the EEC's 30th birthday. Mrs Ros Pyke (72) from Great Barton, Suffolk, stands on top of a Tiger Moth aircraft as it flies over Cranfield Airfield, Beds, and raises £250,000 for charity.
Monday *June 29*	Three young pilot whales called Notch, Tag and Baby, rescued after a mass stranding, are set free in the North Atlantic at Georges Banks, Massachusetts, USA. 30°C in Jersey
Tuesday *June 30*	Army bomb disposal experts defuse a 1016kg World War II bomb near Tower Bridge in London. It contains about 590kg of TNT. All nearby roads are sealed off and 300 people are evacuated. BOMB

TOP TEN TOYS AND BOARD GAMES

	Toys	*Board Games*
1	Sylvanian Families (Toy of the Year)	Trivial Pursuit (Genus II)
2	Lego	A Question of Sport
3	Thundercats	Dingbats
4	Mask	Pictionary
5	Transformers	Balderdash
6	My Little Pony	Quotations
7	Masters of the Universe	Eye
8	Farm Models	Monopoly
9	Barbie	Scrabble
10	Pre-school Toys	Dungeons and Dragons

(from British Toy Retailers Association)

July

Wednesday *July 1*	Belgium hands over the presidency of the EEC to Denmark. 150th birthday of the General Register Office, which became the Office of Population Censuses and Surveys in 1970. So far, it has counted 112,000,000 births, 75,000,000 deaths and 40,000,000 marriages!
Thursday *July 2*	Richard Branson and Per Lindstrand take off from Sugarloaf Mountain, Maine, USA, at dawn to fly across the Atlantic. Their huge black and silver hot-air balloon 'Virgin Atlantic Flyer' is as big as the Albert Hall.
Friday *July 3*	'Virgin Atlantic Flyer' crashes into the Irish Sea near Rathlin Island, off the west coast of Scotland. Richard Branson and Per Lindstrand are rescued by a Royal Navy helicopter from the frigate *Argonaut*.
Saturday *July 4*	American Independence Day. Martina Navratilova beats Steffi Graf 7–5, 6–3 in the Women's Finals at the Wimbledon Lawn Tennis Championships.
Sunday *July 5*	Pat Cash beats Ivan Lendl 7–6, 6–2, 7–5 in the Men's Finals at the Wimbledon Lawn Tennis Championships. 30°C in Cardiff
Monday *July 6*	A competition to build a bridge out of spaghetti is launched by the Department of Civil Engineering at Leeds University. It has to be strong enough to carry a 1kg vehicle over a gap of 300mm using as little spaghetti as possible. Macaroni and lasagne are banned.
Tuesday *July 7*	150th anniversary of the P & O (Peninsula and Orient Steam Navigation Company): the Queen and the Duke of Edinburgh join celebrations on board the 20,000 tonne *Pacific Princess* on the Thames.
Wednesday *July 8*	Huge jellyfish are sighted off the South Coast. Some of them are 1.83m wide and weigh 227.25kg!
Thursday *July 9*	Emergency repairs to the 67,000 tonne QE2's propellers start in King George V dry dock, Southampton. It's the only one in Britain large enough for her!
Friday *July 10*	Queen Mary's Grammar School, Walsall, beats St Paul's, London, in the final of the Times British Schools Chess Championship.

70mm of rain at Girvan, Strathclyde

Full Moon

Saturday *July 11*	Heatwave in the south: 100,000 people haven't got any water in East London and Essex after a blockage develops at the main reservoir in Chigwell. A fleet of 11 water tankers stands by.

July

Named in honour of Julius Caesar. Also known as 'the yellow month' (Gaelic) and 'the month of the midsummer moon' (Anglo-Saxon).

Bird Talk

Albert, the black-browed albatross, arrived back in the Shetlands, as usual, early this year, after months at sea. He was first spotted in the middle of February, back to spend his seventeenth spring and early summer among the gannets at Hermaness, the northern most point on the island of Unst. Each year he comes back to exactly the same spot high on the cliffs at the very top of the British Isles. You can't really miss him with his black eyebrows, long yellow beak and a wingspan of 8ft! Over the years, twitchers have come from far and wide to admire him. This year he leaves a bit earlier than usual—on July 2—to spend the rest of the year at sea.

CLEAN BRITISH BEACHES THAT WIN THE EEC'S BLUE FLAG

Bridlington
Broadstairs
Carnoustie (Tayside)
Crinnis
Fraserburgh (Grampian)
Goodmington
Oddicombe (Devon)
Paignton
Pembray (Dyfed)

Poole Shore Road Sandbanks
Porthmeor (Cornwall)
Porteynon (W. Glamorgan)
Redgate
Southsea (Hants)
Swanage
St Ives
Weymouth

July 21:
PO issues four new stamps to mark the 300th anniversary of the Order of the Thistle

Daily Owl
DEPARTMENT OF ENVIRONMENT SAYS ACID RAIN LEVELS ARE 25% LOWER THAN IN 1980

Sensation
HEATWAVE IN GREECE KILLS 700

News
IT'S OFFICIAL! JAPAN HAS 22 BILLIONAIRES, US ONLY 21

Town Crier
MPS VOTE THEMSELVES A 21·9% PAY RISE, BRINGING THEIR SALARY TO £22,548 A YEAR

Sunday *July 12*	Nigel Mansell wins the British Grand Prix at Silverstone. Queen of the Show at the British Rose Festival, Chiswell Green, Herts, is 'Big Chief', a deep crimson tea rose with very large flowers.
Monday *July 13*	First guided tour of the Bodleian Library, Oxford, for 10 years. It's the oldest public library in Britain, dating from 1602, and houses more than 5,000,000 books!
Tuesday *July 14*	Maurizio Montalbini is brought up to the surface after spending 211 days alone in a cave at Frassasi, Italy: it's a new world record.
Wednesday *July 15*	St Swithin's Day. 78,000 onions roll off a lorry onto a viaduct in The Hague, capital of the Netherlands: special vacuum vehicles suck them up.
Thursday *July 16*	A huge crane lowers a 7.62m oak beam from Windsor Great Park into the ground at the start of the rebuilding of Shakespeare's Globe Theatre in Southwark, East London. It joins other timber posts from Canada, China, Israel, Hungary, America, Portugal, Spain and Russia.
Friday *July 17*	A famous Leonardo da Vinci charcoal drawing of the Madonna and Child is damaged by gun-shot at the National Gallery, London.
Saturday *July 18*	Oxford University refuses Mrs Thatcher, the Prime Minister and an Oxford graduate herself, an honorary degree for the second time.
Sunday *July 19*	Nick Faldo of Great Britain wins the Open Golf Championship at Muirfield, Scotland.
Monday *July 20*	Van Gogh's painting 'Sunflowers', which was bought by a Japanese insurance firm for £24,750,000 in March, goes on show in Tokyo.
Tuesday *July 21*	Daniel Hodes, from California, walks across the Straits of Gibraltar from Africa to Europe in 7hrs wearing huge 3.35m plastic pontoons on each foot.
Wednesday *July 22*	Syria's first astronaut, Lt-Col Muhammad Faris (36), blasts off with two Soviet cosmonauts in a Soyuz TM3 spacecraft, to dock with the orbiting space station *Mir*
Thursday *July 23*	Beginning of Clean Beaches Week: only 17 beaches in Britain win the EEC's Blue Flag.
Friday *July 24*	The *London Daily News*, launched by Robert Maxwell on February 23, closes after its 126th edition.

Saturday *July 25*	The Soviet Union launches a huge space platform into orbit. It's called *Cosmos 1870*, weighs 18 tonnes and circles the Earth every 90 minutes. New Moon 
Sunday *July 26*	Stephen Roche (27), from Dublin, wins the Tour de France in Paris—the first rider from the British Isles ever to win the 27-day race. Opening of the World Wheelchair Games at Stoke Mandeville, Bucks.
Monday *July 27*	Stephane Peyron (26) from France, reaches Brittany after crossing the Atlantic on a 7.62m sailboard. It took him 46 days to cover 6436km from New York to Cap La Rochelle.
Tuesday *July 28*	Laura Davis (23), from Surrey, becomes the first British golfer to win the US Women's Open in New Jersey.
Wednesday *July 29*	Thunderstorms and torrential rain in the South East and East of England. 4.57m floods in Essex. North Weald, nr Epping, is evacuated when the High Street floods. So is a ward at St Margaret's Hospital, Epping. M11 closed between junctions 6 and 7.
Thursday *July 30*	The Queen and the Duke of Edinburgh are the first fare-paying passengers on the new Docklands Light Railway, East London. It costs 40p for a ticket from Poplar to Island Gardens.
Friday *July 31*	More than 80 hot-air balloons take part in Balloon Festival '87 at Southampton. Only 5 manage to land anywhere near the official landing spot for the first race; 1 lands on the roof of Gosport Town Hall!

The British Family 1987

Mr and Mrs 1987 and the little 1987s spend, on average, £9.80 each on food a week. They each drink 4.07 pints of milk and cream a week and eat 4.09oz of cheese, 36.97oz of meat, 5.09oz of fish, 2.89 eggs, 10.04oz of fat and oil, 9.35oz of sugar and preserves, 114.80oz of fresh fruit and vegetables, 54.87oz of bread and cereals and 2.70oz of beverages.

Milk and cream	108.01p
Cheese	34.11p
Meat	292.01p
Fish	52.31p
Eggs	20.60p
Fats and oil	33.37p
Sugar and preserves	17.37p
Fruit and vegetables	212.74p
Bread and cereals	167.87p
Beverages	41.85p
(figures from the National Food Survey)	980.24p = £9.80

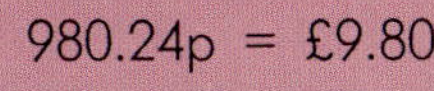

August

Saturday *August 1*	E is the new letter at the beginning of car number plates from today. Royal National Eisteddfod opens in Porthmadog, Wales.
Sunday *August 2*	Teiichi Igarashi (100), reaches the summit of Mount Fuji, Japan (3,775m). It took him 3 days.
Monday *August 3*	Paul Harringan (37), from Morpeth, Northumberland, claims a world record for his leek: it weighs 54.94kg.
Tuesday *August 4*	Choughs or 'Fire Ravens' used to be very common in Cornwall but they stopped breeding there 15 years ago. A special 'Operation Chough' starts today to encourage them back.
Wednesday *August 5*	The Dean of York, the Very Rev John Southgate, flies over the Minster in a hot-air balloon called 'Trinity' to inspect the effects of pollution.
Thursday *August 6*	Ceremony at 8am in Hiroshima, Japan, to mark the 41st anniversary of the dropping of the first atom bomb in 1945.
Friday *August 7*	Lynn Cox (30), from California, swims 4.35km across the Bering Straits from the US to the Soviet Union in 2hrs 12mins. The water, which is frozen for most of the year, is 6°C today! New corn circles appear near the Westbury White Horse, Wilts.
Saturday *August 8*	The Football League's Centenary Match at Wembley: it beats the Rest of the World team 3–0. Full Moon
Sunday *August 9*	Tornado in Rochdale. Lisa Gardner (6) finds a small fragment of dinosaur bone in Hornsleasow Quarry, nr Moreton-in-Marsh, Gloucs.
Monday *August 10*	St Ollie Owl Hospital is opened at Aylesbury, Bucks, by the Wildlife Hospital Trust.
Tuesday *August 11*	Tom McLean, who left Newfoundland on June 16, rows past the Bishop Rock lighthouse, Isles of Scilly, and sets a new world record for crossing the Atlantic in 54days 23hrs.
Wednesday *August 12*	Best night of the year for the Perseid meteor shower—although bright moonlight might spoil the show!
Thursday *August 13*	902.43 hectare 'Watership Down' in Hampshire is sold for £5,000,000. Elton John (real name Reg Dwight) pays £840 for his own Coat of Arms. The motto underneath the shield says 'El tono es bueno' (the music is good).

Friday *August 14*	The elephant trainer's 2 month-old baby daughter is baptised in the ring at Blackpool Tower Circus. It's an ancient tradition for all circus children!
Saturday *August 15*	The National Federation of Zoos launches a 'Parrots in Peril' appeal to save Imperial and Red-Necked parrots.
Sunday *August 16*	The Queen flies to Kirkwall in the Orkneys to celebrate the 850th anniversary of St Magnus Cathedral.
Monday *August 17*	Tom McLean arrives in London after rowing across the Atlantic. Tower Bridge is raised in his honour and *HMS Belfast* fires a 6-gun salute as he rows from St Katherine Dock to London Bridge.

August

Named in honour of the Roman Emperor Augustus, whose lucky month it was. Also known as 'harvest month' and 'weed month'.

Lisa's Bone

'Come on, Lisa, let's go and find a dinosaur,' said Dad and that's just what they do. Lisa Gardner (6), and her father go fossil hunting in Hornsleasow Quarry near their home in Moreton-in-Marsh and find a tiny piece of dinosaur bone measuring about 7.62cm × 6.35cm. They go back to look for more and, on August 27, find four whole vertebrae from the tail of a huge 18m dinosaur called a Cetiosaurus, which means whale lizard! It was a plant-eater which lived 175,000,000 years ago, very like the Apatosaurus or Brontosaurus of North America. Two weeks later, on September 10, they find a tooth belonging to a meat-eating Megalosaurus (big reptile).

As a result of their find, a major dinosaur dig is carried out and 203kg of bones are found, including 25 vertebrae and a 1.5m leg bone! Also, and very importantly, thousands of microfossils are discovered by sieving the clay, revealing crocodile teeth, fish scales, turtles' shells, wing bones from flying reptiles and the earliest known salamander.

Tuesday *August 18*	Philip Rush (23) from New Zealand, swims the English Channel three ways in 28 hours 21 minutes, breaking the record by 10 hours and 6 minutes.
Wednesday *August 19*	Priddy Sheep Fair takes place on the Green at Priddy near Wells, Somerset. It's always held on the third Wednesday in August.
Thursday *August 20*	An expedition to climb Xixa-bangma (8047m), China's highest peak, is mounted by Col John Blashford-Snell.
Friday *August 21*	An Islander aircraft crash lands on Formby Beach, Southport, Merseyside, at 6.30am. The pilot tries to dig it out but the tide washes it away. *30.02°C at Liphook, Hants*
Saturday *August 22*	Storms and floods all over the country. Hailstones bigger than marbles dent cars and smash windows in Woodbridge, Suffolk.
Sunday *August 23*	The 'Famous Five' series by Enid Blyton comes top in a survey of the most popular books for 10–11 year olds in Wales.
Monday *August 24*	St Bartholomew's Day. Dogs for Disabled scheme is launched in London. *New Moon*
Tuesday *August 25*	Floods in the south of England. Forest fires in the south of France. *13°C in London*
Wednesday *August 26*	Islamic New Year (AH 1408). An Abyssinian spotted owl, stolen from London Zoo three weeks ago, is found and returned safely.
Thursday *August 27*	Rory Blackwell (54) from Devon breaks the world one-man marching band record by walking 24.14km and playing 26 instruments.
Friday *August 28*	The RSPB says that red kites have had their best year for a century, successfully raising 38 fledglings in central Wales.
Saturday *August 29*	Warning: a savage 3.66m conger eel is attacking fishermen and swimmers at Gosport, Hampshire. It's also been sighted in waters around Portsmouth Harbour.
Sunday *August 30*	The Notting Hill Carnival in London. Ben Johnson (Canada) becomes the fastest man in the world. He breaks the 100m record at the World Athletics Championships in Rome in a time of 9.83secs—one tenth of a second faster than the previous record.
Monday *August 31*	Bank Holiday. The Docklands Light Railway in London opens to the public. It should have opened a month ago.

September

Tuesday *September 1*	A cloud of black gas sweeps over Kent from Ramsgate to Herne Bay: 23 people are taken to hospital with skin rashes, stinging eyes and sore throats. 

Wednesday *September 2*	A 6.1m whale, stuck in the mud at Beachley, Gloucs, is pushed back into the River Severn by coastguards. 
Thursday *September 3*	NASA scientists celebrate the 10th anniversary of the launching of *Voyager 2* spacecraft. It's now over 5631.5 million km from Earth, on its way to Neptune.
Friday *September 4*	The Blackpool Illuminations are switched on at 9pm: they stretch for 9.5km along the front.
Saturday *September 5*	Don Allum (50), lands at Achill Island, off the west coast of Ireland, and becomes the first man to row the Atlantic in both directions! It took him 76 days to cross from Newfoundland in his 6.1m boat *QE3*. 
Sunday *September 6*	Fatima Whitbread (26), throws a javelin 76.64m at the World Athletic Championships in Rome and wins a gold medal.
Monday *September 7*	One of the largest sailing ships in the world, the *Amerigo Vespucci*, named after the famous Italian navigator, is moored next to the *Cutty Sark* at Greenwich. It's on a 6-day visit as part of European Year of the Environment. 

Tuesday *September 8*	Widecombe Fair is held at Widecombe-in-the-Moor, Dartmoor, Devon: it's always held on the second Tuesday of September.
Wednesday *September 9*	A service is held in St Etienne's Church in Caen, Normandy, to inaugurate a new tomb containing the left thigh bone of William the Conqueror. It was the only bit of him that was left when his original wooden coffin was opened in 1983. 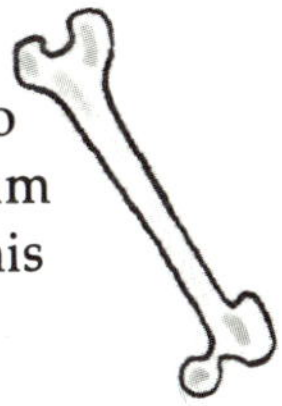
Thursday *September 10*	The body of a 11.26m leather-backed turtle, washed up on the island of Lewis, Outer Hebrides, is put back in the Atlantic: the Receiver of Wreck had offered it to the British Museum but they didn't want it.
Friday *September 11*	144-year-old Nelson, on top of his column in Trafalgar Square, London, is injected with resin to fill up his cracks.
Saturday *September 12*	Pick your own apples this weekend in the Queen's orchards at Sandringham. Third National Bat Conference opens in Durham. 

Sunday *September 13*	Chris Farrant, from Ottery St Mary, Devon, claims a world record with an onion that weighs 4.196kg. It is 68.58cm round the middle!

68.58cm

Monday *September 14*	The Day of the Holy Nut: beginning of the nutting season. All performances at the Royal Opera House in London are cancelled until further notice after the chorus rejects a new pay offer.
Tuesday *September 15*	The Duchess of York takes her first helicopter lesson at RAF Benson, Oxfordshire. 25th European and 4th World Sand Yacht Championships start at Lytham St Anne's, Lancashire.
Wednesday *September 16*	Prince Harry (3yrs 1day) starts nursery school in Notting Hill, London: he makes a pair of cardboard binoculars. European rocket *Ariane* is launched from French Guiana.
Thursday *September 17*	The Prince of Wales climbs the 123.14m spire of Salisbury Cathedral to lay the first stone at the beginning of restoration work costing £6,500,000.

Friday *September 18*	A 7.5 tonne yacht called *Panacea*, beached on rocks near Kimmeridge, Dorset, is lifted by helicopter and flown to the Isle of Wight!
Saturday *September 19*	A 2-year-old ferret called Salt wins the World Champion title beating 80 other contestants in Eye, Suffolk. It's 27 years since the first parking tickets were issued in London!
Sunday *September 20*	Alain Prost wins the Portuguese Grand Prix—his 28th World Championship! The Swan's Way, a 105km bridleway from Salcey Forest, Northants, to Goring, Oxfordshire, is opened today.
Monday *September 21*	Durham Cathedral and Castle are listed as a World Heritage Site: a time capsule is buried on Palace Green to mark the occasion.
Tuesday *September 22*	200 cartoons are entered in the Dog Cartoonist of the Year Competition in London.

New Moon

Wednesday *September 23*	Betty's Tea Shop, Northallerton, N. Yorks, wins the 'Top Tea Place of the Year' Gold Award from the Tea Council.
Thursday *September 24*	Jewish New Year (AM 5748). The Pilgrims' Way, linking Holy Island to the mainland, is re-opened after repairs. St Stephen's Walbrook, in the City of London, re-opens after £1,300,000 restoration. It's got a new marble altar by the sculptor Henry Moore.

September

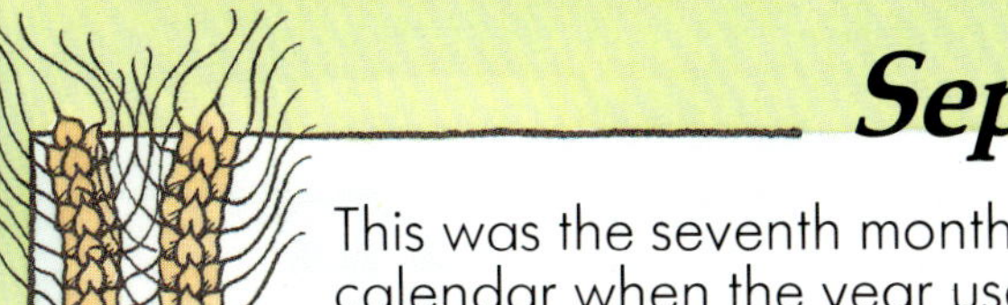
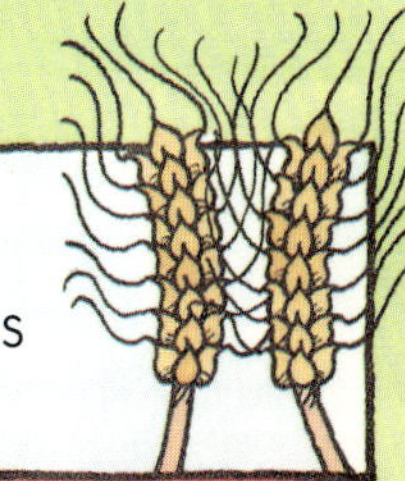

This was the seventh month of the year in the old Roman calendar when the year used to start in March. Also known as the 'month of reaping', 'barley month' and the 'holy month'.

September 8: PO issues four new stamps to celebrate the 150th anniversary of Queen Victoria's accession to the throne

Durham Castle and Cathedral

Durham Castle was built in 1069, just after the Norman Conquest. The Cathedral, finished in 1133, is a shrine to St Cuthbert, and is the finest Norman building in the whole of Europe. Other world heritage sites in Britain are: Fountains Abbey; Studley Royal; Stonehenge; Avebury; Ironbridge Gorge Museum; The Welsh Castles and Town Walls of Edward I; St Kilda; Giant's Causeway in Northern Ireland

Beacon

MORE THAN 24 MILLION PEOPLE HOMELESS IN BANGLADESH AFTER WORST FLOODS EVER.

Daily Scroll

23,000 YEAR OLD PREHISTORIC BOOMERANG FOUND IN POLAND

The Bug

BIGGEST IRON AGE BURIAL SITE IN BRITAIN FOUND IN YORKSHIRE

Neptune

VENOMOUS TRINIDAD CHEVRON SPIDER FOUND IN BOX OF BANANAS AT NEWQUAY

Friday *September 25*	Ten Germans abseil down Tower Bridge, London, in protest at North Sea pollution.

Saturday *September 26*	A 9.144m whale is spotted off Canvey Island, Essex, heading up the River Thames towards London!
Sunday *September 27*	Emil Zatopek, who won gold medals at the Olympics in 1948 and 1952, takes part in the *Sunday Times* Fun Run in Hyde Park, London: so do 32,000 other runners.

Monday *September 28*	The Duchess of York plants a spice tree in the gardens of an old sugar plantation in Mauritius, which is now used as a museum.
Tuesday *September 29*	Topping In ceremony at Seven Dials, Covent Garden, London. An airtight time capsule is buried in the foundations of a new monument, which is being built to replace the 17th-century one.
Wednesday *September 30*	A 300-year-old wooden doll is sold for £26,400 at Phillips, London. A new electronic speed trap starts work on the Severn Bridge today to enforce the 40mph/64.36kph limit.

Champions of 1987

Toymaker of the Year	Brian Nicholls
Independent Railway of the Year	Bluebell Line
Businesswoman of the Year	Jenifer Rosenberg
Miss England	Debbie Pearman
World Champion Ferret	Salt
Museum of the Year	Manchester Museum
Brain of Britain	Ian Sutton
Cruft's Champion	Viscount Grant (Gable)
Smithfield Supreme Cattle Champion	Ebor Ricky
Miss World	Miss Austria (Ulla Weigerstorfer)
British Monopoly Champion	Mike Grabsky
Doctor of the Year	Dr John Pickup
Scrabble Champion	Nigel Ingham
Top Tea Place of the Year	Betty's Tea Shop, Northallerton, Yorks
Miss Universe	Cecilia Bolocco
Times Crossword Puzzle Champion	William Pilkington
Mastermind	Dr Jeremy Bradbrooke
World Eel Eating Champion	Mark Ryder

October

Thursday *October 1*	The Soviet cosmonaut Yuri Romanenko breaks the record for human endurance in space after spending 237 days orbiting Earth.
Friday *October 2*	Archaeologists announce that the tomb of Queen Eurydice, grandmother of Alexander the Great, has been found below Mount Olympus in northern Greece. It dates from 330BC.
Saturday *October 3*	Sven Voss (9), from West Germany, wins first prize in the Rubik Olympics in London. A colony of badgers gets a 61cm high underpass in Penzance, Cornwall.
Sunday *October 4*	A high-rise block called Wishford Point, on the Trowbridge Estate, Hackney, is demolished with 227kg of nitro-glycerine.
Monday *October 5*	Hundreds of twitchers flock to Blakeney Point and Wells, on the north Norfolk coast, to see an olive-backed pipit and a dusky warbler. They're rare birds from Siberia, blown off course by strong east winds while they were migrating!
Tuesday *October 6*	The giant Channel Tunnel drill is put together 40m below the sea near Dover. It weighs 609.6 tonnes and is 182.9m long. Full Moon
Wednesday *October 7*	Gales uproot trees and bring down power cables in the south of England. Roads in Kent, Sussex and Hampshire are flooded.
Thursday *October 8*	A black and white warbler, blown across the Atlantic by gales, is spotted at Prawle Point, Devon.
Friday *October 9*	Torrential rain and gales. Snow falls at Alwen, Clywd. Start of 'Operation Deepscan' to find the Loch Ness Monster: 20 boats take part.
Saturday *October 10*	Torrential rain and gales in the south of England: Essex is worst hit with Finchingfield, Great Yeldham and Steeple Bumpstead flooded. Firemen rescue 150 cows trapped by 91.5m of water in a milking parlour at Rushall, Norfolk.
Sunday *October 11*	'Operation Deepscan' finishes without finding the Loch Ness Monster.
Monday *October 12*	Start of Dyslexia Week. Mrs Linda Withers from Brothertoft, near Boston, Lincs, wins the British National Pumpkin Championships at Ashby-de-la-Zouch, Leics. Her entry weighs 128.93kg!
Tuesday *October 13*	42 pilot whales beach themselves at Waihou Bay on the east coast of New Zealand. Rescuers manage to save 30 of them by pushing them out to sea.

| *Wednesday*
October 14 | The Britannia gold bullion coin goes on sale for the first time: there are four sizes—1oz, ½oz, ¼oz, and ¹⁄₁₀oz (28.35g/14.17g/7.09g/2.83g). |

| *Thursday*
October 15 | Flood Warning in the south east of England. Bob Geldof receives an honorary degree from the Princess Royal, Chancellor of London University. |

| *Friday*
October 16 | **The Great Storm:** hurricane force winds destroy more than 15,000,000 trees in the south of England and 13 people are killed. There is a massive black-out in London. |

| *Saturday*
October 17 | A clouded leopard, which escaped from a zoo nr Canterbury when a tree crushed its cage during the storm yesterday, is still on the loose! A rare hoard of Iron Age coins is found in Essex. |

| *Sunday*
October 18 | A huge iceberg, 159.3km long and 46.66 wide, breaks away from the Ross Ice Shelf in the Antarctic. It will take about 10yrs to melt. |

| *Monday*
October 19 | Black Monday on London's Stock Exchange: it's the worst day for shares this century as their value drops by £50 billion. |

| *Tuesday*
October 20 | More floods in the south: nearly 2.5cm of rain falls in London between 9pm and midnight. |

| *Wednesday*
October 21 | Trafalgar Day. Sir Stanley Matthews (72), who played football for England and Stoke, unveils a life-size statue of himself in Stoke-on-Trent. New Moon |

| *Thursday*
October 22 | The first American yellow-billed cuckoo ever sighted in Britain is spotted at Rauceby, Lincs. |

| *Friday*
October 23 | Mount Everest is definitely the highest mountain in the world, after being re-measured by satellite receivers. It's precisely 8863m and K2 is only 8607m! |

| *Saturday*
October 24 | 51 herds of cattle in the south of England are suffering from a new disease – Bovine Spongiform Encephalopathy or Mad Cow Disease. |

| *Sunday*
October 25 | St Crispin's Day. Big Ben isn't working because of a crack in the chiming mechanism. |

Monday *October 26*	Hundreds of twitchers flock to Lundy Island in the Bristol Channel to see a North American veery (a thrush-like bird), blown across the Atlantic by gales.
Tuesday *October 27*	The Prince of Wales launches the Wishing Well Appeal to raise £30,000,000 for the Hospital for Sick Children, Great Ormond Street, London.
Wednesday *October 28*	The north part of Kew Gardens, London, re-opens 12 days after the storm. Over 1000 trees were blown down. 
Thursday *October 29*	A gas cloud from a chemical plant in SW France drifts towards the coast of Devon and Cornwall.
Friday *October 30*	The London newspaper *The Evening News* closes today, after the circulation drops to 39,000. The £25,000,000 William Herschel Telescope on La Palma, in the Canary Islands, starts operating.
Saturday *October 31*	Hallowe'en. It's been the fourth wettest October in England and Wales since 1727!

October

This was the eighth month in the old Roman calendar when the year started in March. It's also been known as 'wine month' and 'month of the winter moon'.

The Great Wind

October's hurricane roars in from the Atlantic at 177km/h and destroys millions of trees in southern England, cutting a path of devastation across the country. Many of the trees had taken hundreds of years to grow and are irreplaceable, like the 33.5m mulberry tree planted outside King's School, Canterbury, in the reign of King James I, or many of the rare specimens at Kew Gardens, London, which altogether loses a third of its trees during the storm. Six of the seven oak trees, which give Sevenoaks in Kent its name, are blown down.

Lots of important buildings are badly damaged including Chichester and Portsmouth Cathedrals. Selfridge's windows in Oxford Street, London, blow in as well!

October 13: PO issues four new stamps 'Studio Pottery'

November

Sunday *November 1*	A De Dion Bouton tricycle, made in 1898, wins the London to Brighton Veteran Car Run in 2.5hrs. 306 of the 380 entrants finish.
Monday *November 2*	The annual Poppy Appeal is launched in Whitehall. Fruit growers ask for Government help: the hurricane last month blew down 250,000 fruit trees and damaged 500,000: altogether, about 14,500 tonnes of fruit was ruined.
Tuesday *November 3*	Captain Michael Hill of the Royal Artillery pops a champagne cork 33.35m at the Oval, London, and claims a world record.
Wednesday *November 4*	The European Community takes emergency measures against swarms of locusts reaching Europe from North Africa.
Thursday *November 5*	Guy Fawkes Night (1605). The Archbishop of Canterbury, Dr Robert Runcie, is winched 9.14m in the air by a Royal Navy helicopter from a Falmouth lifeboat in a practice 'rescue' operation off the coast of Cornwall.
Friday *November 6*	The Victoria and Albert Museum in London opens on a Friday for the first time since 1977.
Saturday *November 7*	Parade in Red Square, Moscow, to mark the 70th anniversary of the Russian Revolution. The BTR 80, the Soviet Union's newest amphibious armoured personnel carrier, is shown for the first time.
Sunday *November 8*	Remembrance Sunday: two minutes silence is observed at 11am. A bomb explodes during a service at Enniskillen, Co Fermanagh: 11 people are killed and 61 injured.
Monday *November 9*	Winter Carnival at Highbridge and Burnham-on-Sea, Somerset, with an illuminated procession through the town.
Tuesday *November 10*	Dumfries wins BR's 'Best Station' competition. Best small station is Templecombe, Somerset, and the staff at Carlisle station win the prize for being nice to customers.
Wednesday *November 11*	Armistice Day: it's a National Holiday in France, where people wear cornflowers instead of poppies. Van Gogh's 'Irises' is sold for a record £30,200,000 at Sotheby's, New York.
Thursday *November 12*	Miss Austria, Ulla Weigerstorfer (20), wins Miss World at the Royal Albert Hall. The runners-up are Miss Venezuela and Miss Iceland.

November

This was the ninth month in the old Roman calendar when the year started in March. It's also been known as 'wind month', 'slaughter month' and 'the month of blood'.

To qualify for a commemorative plaque you have to be very famous, to have made an important contribution to human happiness or to deserve recognition. You also have to be dead for at least 20 years!

Other blue plaques to famous people put up in London this year include:

Amy Johnson (1903–1941)
Aviator
Vernon Court, Hendon Way,
NW2

Nancy Astor (1879–1964)
First woman MP
4 St James's Square, SW1

Isaac Rosenberg
(1890–1918) Poet and
Painter
77 Whitechapel High St, E1

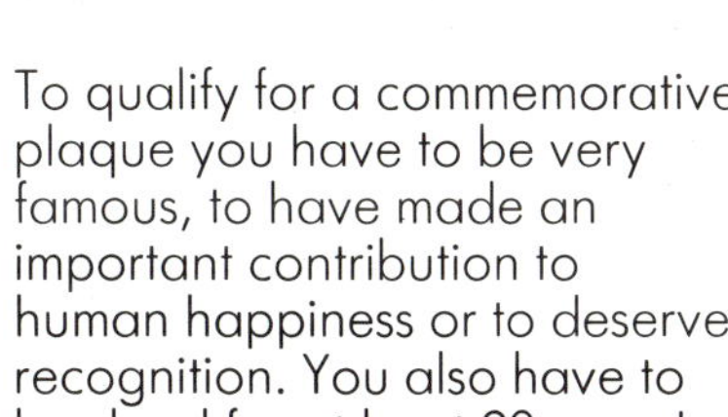

November 18: *King's Cross Fire*

Fire sweeps through King's Cross underground station in London, killing 30 people. It is the worst accident ever on the London Underground, and is instrumental in the banning of smoking anywhere on the underground system.

November 17:
PO issues five new
Christmas stamps

Friday *November 13*	The third Friday the Thirteenth this year! Members of the Friday the 13th Club in Philadelphia, USA, sit down to a banquet of fried grasshoppers and roasted caterpillars. Afterwards they spill salt, open umbrellas indoors and walk under ladders!
Saturday *November 14*	Lord Mayor's Show in London: six Shire horses pull the new Lord Mayor, Alderman Sir Greville Spratt, his wife and chaplain, in his golden coach.
Sunday *November 15*	Duncan Goodhew, the Olympic swimming champion, launches the 'Swimathon' in aid of the Children's Hospital in Great Ormond Street, London, at the Queen Mother's Sports Centre, Westminster.
Monday *November 16*	The Open College of the Arts is launched today. A Blue Plaque is unveiled at St Mark's Vicarage, 52 Kennington Oval, London, today to mark the birthplace of Field Marshal Viscount Montgomery of Alamein.
Tuesday *November 17*	Experts from Gloucester City Museum visit a quarry in Moreton-in-Marsh, where vertebrae and a tooth belonging to a 180,000,000-year-old dinosaur have been found.
Wednesday *November 18*	Prince Edward switches on the Christmas lights in Regent Street, London.
Thursday *November 19*	A 1931 Bugatti Type 41 Sports Coupe is auctioned by Christie's for £5,500,000—the largest amount ever paid for a vintage car!
Friday *November 20*	The Queen and the Duke of Edinburgh's Ruby Wedding Anniversary: they've been married for 40 years! Elton John sells Watford Football Club to Robert Maxwell for £2,000,000.

Saturday *November 21*	Mohamed Al-Fayed, who owns Harrods, welcomes Father Christmas as he arrives in his grotto. New Moon
Sunday *November 22*	Stir-Up Sunday: time to make the Christmas Puddings! The Pope beatifies 85 Roman Catholic martyrs, who were hung, drawn and quartered between 1584 and 1679 in England.
Monday *November 23*	The Trafalgar Square Christmas tree begins its journey from Norway to England, on the back of a lorry. It's an annual present from the people of Oslo to the people of London.

Tuesday *November 24*	Smoking is banned everywhere in the London Underground system.
Wednesday *November 25*	*HMS Endurance* sets sail for the Falkland Islands to look for 300 King Penguin eggs which will be taken to Sea World, San Diego, California.

Thursday *November 26*	Flood Warnings in Venice and Florence, Italy: soldiers deliver sand bags to art galleries while precious paintings are moved to top floors in Florence. There's 20.32cm of water in St Mark's Square, Venice.
Friday *November 27*	An earth tremor shakes Sussex from Bognor Regis to Crawley: it's caused by movement in the Chichester Fault, which runs under the south of England from Guildford right out into the English Channel.
Saturday *November 28*	Sheffield will host the 1991 World Student Games: the first time that the event has ever been held in Britain. –10°C at St Harmon, Powys
Sunday *November 29*	Young pilgrims walk 96.54km from Canterbury Cathedral to St George the Martyr Church, Southwark, London, to raise money for homeless people.
Monday *November 30*	St Andrew's Day. The wild cat, the dormouse, and the Lundy cabbage are among 48 species of animals and 31 species of plants to get protection under the Wildlife and Countryside Act.

Some of the animals and plants to get protection when the Wildlife and Countryside Act is reviewed

Ivell's Sea Anemone	Marine Turtles	Grass-poly
Startlet Sea Anemone	Vendace	Stinking Hawk's-beard
Apus	Walrus	Young's Helleborine
Violet Click Beetle	Whale	Branched Horsetail
Wild Cat	Whitefish	Green Hound's-tongue
New Forest Cicada		Creeping Marshwort
Dormouse	Lundy Cabbage	Cambridge Milk-parsley
Medicinal Leech	Purple Colt's-foot	Pennyroyal
Pine Marten	Slender Cottongrass	Pigmyweed
Trembling Sea Mat	Sand Crocus	Small Restharrow
Viper's Bugloss Moth	Alpine Fleabane	Fingered Speedwell
Lagoon Sandworm	Small Fleabane	Strapwort
Fairy Shrimp	Fringed Gentian	Viper's-grass
Lagoon Sand Shrimp	Stinking Goosefoot	

PS The Carthusian snail and the Chequered Skipper butterfly get taken OFF the list of protected creatures because they are more common than previously thought!

December

Tuesday *December 1*	A 12.19m × 3.05m model train set goes on display at Eurotunnel's offices in London: it shows the British end of the Channel Tunnel at Folkestone, complete with trains built on a scale of 1:160.
Wednesday *December 2*	The bones of four 12,800-year-old mammoths, found in a gravel pit at Condover, Shropshire, are put into temporary storage while the jaws and teeth are treated at Oxford. They will all go on show at Cosford Aerospace Museum, north Shropshire.
Thursday *December 3*	The Princess of Wales helps Father Christmas to give out presents at the Children's Hospital, Great Ormond Street, London.
Friday *December 4*	The Duke of Edinburgh cuts the ribbon and officially opens the Imperial Archway in Chinatown, Manchester. Full Moon
Saturday *December 5*	Watch out for the Bradford comet which has appeared low above the western horizon. It's the brightest since Halley's!
Sunday *December 6*	The Feast of St Nicholas. Six new oak saplings are planted at Sevenoaks, Kent, to replace the trees that were blown down in October's hurricane. The town has had a line of seven oak trees since 700AD!
Monday *December 7*	London's Greatest Traffic Jam ever starts at 4.34pm when a lorry, a coach and a car collide at the entrance to Blackfriars underpass. By 7pm there are about 50,000 vehicles gridlocked from Hampstead in the north to Wimbledon in the south!
Tuesday *December 8*	President Reagan and Mikhail Gorbachev sign a treaty agreeing to scrap all medium and short-range nuclear missiles. More traffic chaos in London: the traffic lights computer fails at Trafalgar Square.
Wednesday *December 9*	Prince Harry (3), wearing a green tunic, red tights and a bobble hat, appears as a goblin in his school play *The Special Little Christmas Tree*.
Thursday *December 10*	The Christmas Tree lights in Trafalgar Square are switched on by the Mayor of Oslo, Albert Nordengen. Two protestors, who climb to the top of the tree with a banner saying 'Stop Acid Rain', are removed by the London Fire Brigade.
Friday *December 11*	European astronomers are given the go-ahead for the world's largest telescope: it will take ten years to build and will be called the Very Large Telescope (VLT).
Saturday *December 12*	The Great Christmas Pudding Race is held in Covent Garden, London: children's race starts at 10.30am, adults' at 11am.

Sunday *December 13*	The first ships which left Portsmouth 213 days ago, retracing the voyage of the first settlers to Australia, arrive in Fremantle.
Monday *December 14*	Busiest day for the Christmas Post: 105,000,000 cards, parcels and letters are posted today!
Tuesday *December 15*	On show in London is an army of life-sized terracotta warriors and horses from China. They're 2000yrs old and were made to guard the tomb of Emperor Qin Shiluang.
Wednesday *December 16*	The House of Lords debates the pelicans in St James' Park: no eggs have been laid since the reign of James I!
Thursday *December 17*	The Chancellor of the Exchequer, Nigel Lawson, announces that smaller 5p and 10p coins are going to be introduced.
Friday *December 18*	End of term for the House of Commons! Members of Parliament break up for their three-week Christmas holiday today.
Saturday *December 19*	A VC10 aircraft, carrying 1360.8kg of Christmas mail, makes the fastest non-stop flight from Britain to the Falkland Islands in 15hrs, 45mins and 10secs. New Moon
Sunday *December 20*	Christmas Water Carnival at Bristol. Canon John Morris holds a special service to bless animals in Battersea Hippodrome at 3pm.

December

This used to be the tenth month in the old Roman calendar when the year started in March.

The Pannage Season for Pigs

If you happen to wander through the New Forest in Hampshire one autumn, you might meet the odd pink pig trotting through the leaves, looking rather full. Don't worry, it's only the Pannage Season, when farmers are allowed to turn out their pigs into the forest to eat all the acorns and beech nuts which give the ponies and cattle who live there extremely bad stomach aches. This year, in fact, the problem has been so bad that the Court of Verderers, which controls such things, grants a special extension of the season until December 31, so that the pigs can munch their way through Christmas right up to New Year's Eve!

Monday *December 21*	200 hippies celebrate the Winter Solstice at dawn at Stonehenge. The largest trawler built in Britain for 10 years, the 39.01m *Thornella*, is launched sideways into the River Ouse at Selby, Yorks.
Tuesday *December 22*	Shortest day of the year. A rare American bald eagle, found in the Irish Republic after being blown across the Atlantic by strong winds, flies back to New York first class, courtesy of Aer Lingus. 
Wednesday *December 23*	Three Soviet cosmonauts, launched on Monday from the Baikonur cosmodrome, dock with the orbiting space station *Mir*. They will replace Yuri Romanenko and Alexander Alexandrov.
Thursday *December 24*	Christmas Eve. The Post Office delivers a record 1,488,000,000 letters and cards this Christmas! More than 330,000 children have written to Father Christmas.
Friday *December 25*	Christmas Day. 10,000,000 turkeys are eaten today and, on average, each child gets between £70 and £80 of presents!
Saturday *December 26*	Boxing Day. The annual pilgrimage from Ripon Cathedral to Fountains Abbey starts at 11am. *The Times* newspaper is published on Boxing Day for the first time.
Sunday *December 27*	13°C in south west and central England: it's so warm that jellyfish have been spotted off the north coast of Wales!
Monday *December 28*	The statue of Winston Churchill in Parliament Square, London, is floodlit for the first time.
Tuesday *December 29*	Yuri Romanenko returns to Earth in a *Soyuz TM-3* space capsule and lands on the snowy steppes 1995km south east of Moscow. He has spent a record-breaking 326 days in space and has grown 1cm.
Wednesday *December 30*	Mrs Thatcher plans a party at No 10 Downing Street this weekend to celebrate becoming the longest continuous serving Prime Minister this century.
Thursday *December 31*	A 'leap second' is added on to the end of 1987 to bring clocks into line with the Earth's rotation. A World Wildlife Fund report says that at least 1000 species, mainly insects, became extinct in 1987.